GODS AND GODDESSES

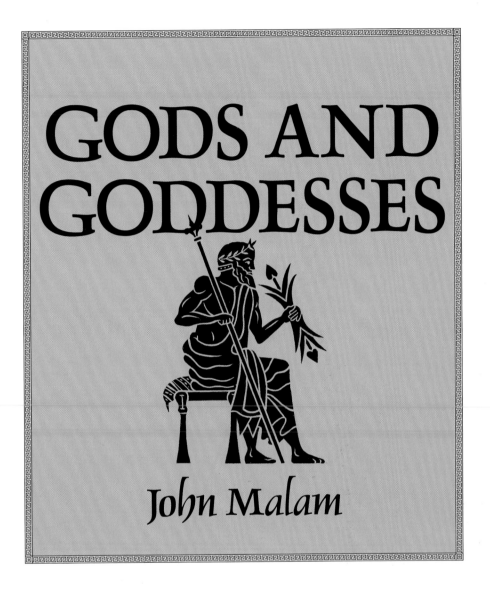

John Malam

PETER BEDRICK BOOKS
INCORPORATED

ANCIENT GREECE
Daily Life
Gods and Goddesses
Greek Theatre
The Original Olympics

Published in the United States in 1999 by
Peter Bedrick Books
A division of NTC/Contemporary Publishing Group, Inc.
4255 West Touhy Avenue,
Lincolnwood (Chicago), Illinois 60646-1975 U.S.A.

Photographic acknowldgements
The publishers wish to thank the following sources for providing photographs:
AKG London 7, 15, 17 (top, left), 19, 21, 32, 39, 40; **Bridgeman/ Birmingham Museum and Art Gallery** 2; **Staatlich Museum, Berlin** 36; **C. M. Dixon** 5, 6, 8, 12, 17 (right), 18, 22, 25, 26, 29, 30, 35 (top), 41, 42, 43; **e t archive** (cover), 10, 11; **Mary Evans** 31; **Werner Forman** 34; **Michael Holford** 16, 23; **Billie Love** 27; John Malam 45; **Wayland Picture Library** 13; **British Museum** (contents), 33.
Illustration: John Yates **Map designs:** Hardlines

Malam, John.

    Gods and Goddesses / John Malam.

       p.   cm. --   (Ancient Greece)

    Includes bibliographical references and index.

    Summary: Discusses the important gods and goddesses of ancient Greece and retells some of the myths about them, including Zeus, Hera, Athena, and Hades.

    ISBN 0-87226-598-6 (hc)

    1. Mythology, Greek Juvenile literature.   [1. Mythology, Greek.]

I. Title. II. Series : Ancient Greece (Peter Bedrick Books)

BL.M25   1999

292.2'11--dc21
                                    99-11849
                                       CIP

Printed and bound by Eurografica, Italy
International Standard Book Number: 0-87226-598-6

99 00 01 02 03 15 14 13 12 11 10 9 8 7 6 5 4 3 2 1

CONTENTS

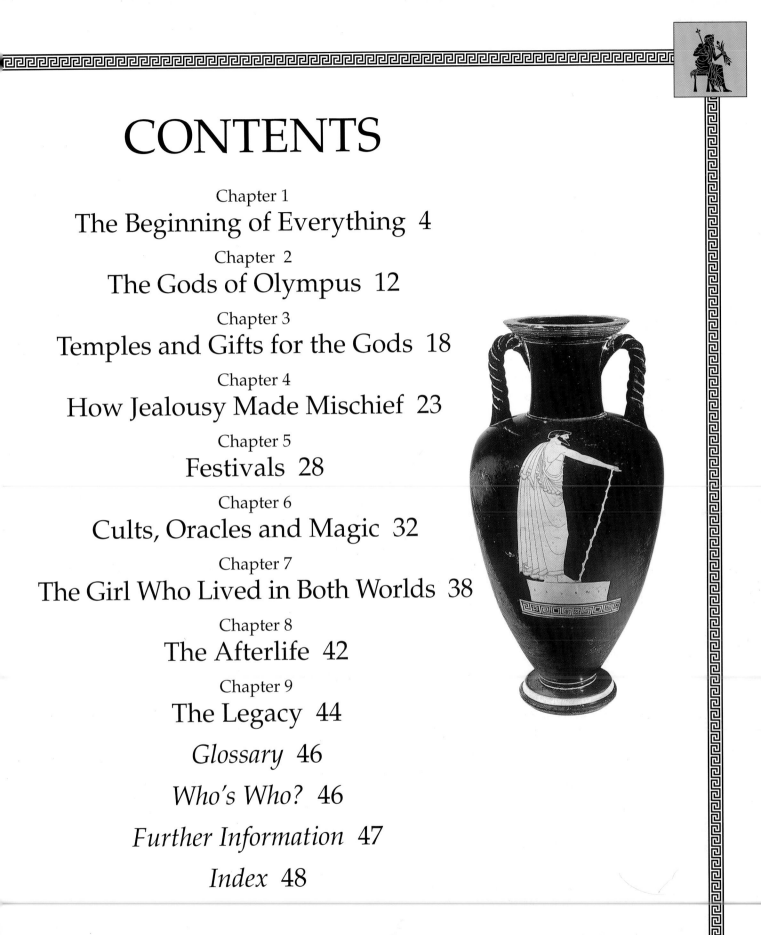

1 The Beginning of Everything

Long ago, at the beginning of time itself, there was nothing but Chaos. The world as we know it did not exist. No land. No sky. No sea. Not a thing.

Then, out of the darkness that was Chaos came light, and Mother Earth and Sky were born. They produced twelve children, supernatural beings called the Titans, who were the first gods to rule the world.

The birth of Zeus

Two of the Titans, Cronos and Rhea, had children – but Cronos was afraid of them and refused to let them live. As each child was born, he swallowed it – all except for the last born, a boy, whom Rhea gave birth to in secret.

Rhea wanted her child to live. She entrusted the baby to the safekeeping of Mother Earth, who carried him off to the island of Crete. The child was called Zeus.

This map shows the major religious sites in the ancient Greek world and the gods and goddesses who were worshiped there.

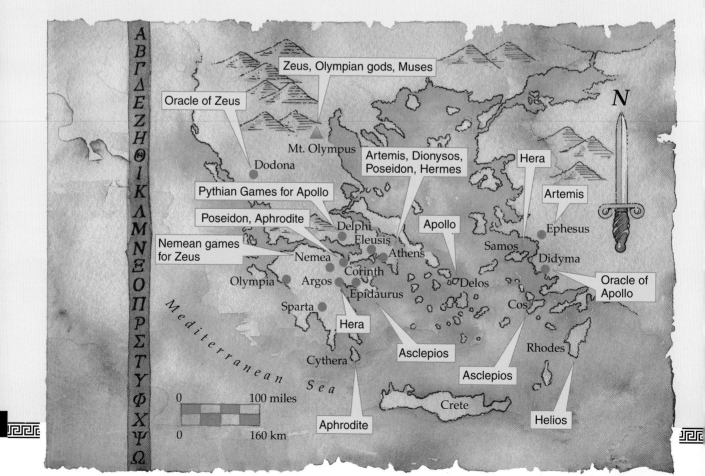

Why was Cronos afraid of his own children? He had been warned by Mother Earth that one of them would become the most important god of all – a god among gods, king of all things and greater even than Cronos himself. Cronos was troubled. Surely, he thought, if he killed his children as each was born, he would have nothing to fear from them.

Cronos was wrong, since Mother Earth had not told him everything. She had not warned him that Rhea would trick him. Instead of handing over baby Zeus to be eaten, Rhea passed Cronos a rock wrapped in swaddling clothes. Cronos swallowed it, believing that he was swallowing his newborn child.

On Crete, baby Zeus was safe. He grew strong, cared for by *nymphs* who fed him on milk and honey.

Zeus as the god of weather:

"Zeus, son of Cronos, god of the dark clouds, who is lord of all."

From the poem *Odyssey*, written down by Homer, c. 750 BC.

ΣΤΥΦΧΨ

ΟΠΡΣΤΥΦΧΨΩ

A metal statue of Zeus, the king of the Olympian gods. He is about to throw a thunderbolt with his right hand, while in his outstretched left hand he holds a bird to show that he ruled over the sky.

Zeus' brothers and sisters were set free

There came a time when Cronos was fooled again. Zeus, by now grown up, became *cupbearer* to Cronos, who did not know that it was his own son who brought him cups of wine each day.

One day, Zeus mixed poison into the wine, and at once Cronos was sick. He spat out the rock, followed by his children, whose names were Demeter, Hades, Hera, Hestia, and Poseidon. And this is how the brothers and sisters of Zeus, born for a second time, were free at last from the prison of their father's belly.

The struggle against the Titans

In the far north of Greece is the mountain, *Mount Olympus*, and it was here that Zeus lived with his brothers and sisters. They were called the Olympians – which means the gods of Mount Olympus – all except for Hades, who was never thought of as one of them.

For ten years, the Olympians, helped by Hades, fought the Titans to decide who should rule the world. Floods, earthquakes, and droughts ravaged the earth.

Only when the one-eyed monsters called Cyclopes joined forces with the Olympians did the struggle end. The Cyclopes gave the Olympians the tools to defeat the Titans. They armed Zeus with the *thunderbolt*, Poseidon with the *trident*, and Hades with the hat of darkness. These gifts became their symbols from then on.

While the young Zeus lived on Crete, he hid in a cave where his father, Cronos, would not find him. This is the Diktean cave, believed by the ancient Greeks to be the birthplace of Zeus.

Wearing his hat of darkness, Hades crept unseen into Cronos' dwelling place on *Mount Othrys* and hid Cronos' weapons. Then, Poseidon came at him with his trident, and Zeus filled the air with the noise of thunder and the flash of lightning. The Titans fled and were chased by the Olympians into *Tartarus*, a place deep inside the earth from which there was no escape.

Of the Titans, only Atlas was spared from being imprisoned in Tartarus. For his punishment, he was made to carry the weight of the heavens on his shoulders for all time. His seven daughters were changed into stars called the Pleiades. To this day, they shine brightly in the night sky, held there by their father, Atlas.

The punishment of Atlas:

"Atlas holds up the wide heaven with unwearying head and arms, standing at the borders of the earth. This is how wise Zeus punished him."

From the poem *Theogony*, written by Hesiod, c. 700 BC.

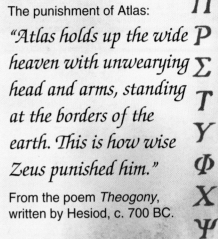

The Olympian gods fought against a race of Giants, too. Here, Poseidon (on the left) attacks the giant Ephialtes with his three-pronged trident, while at the same time crushing him with a piece of the earth.

The creation of humankind

The Olympian gods now ruled the earth, and Zeus set about creating a race of people to live there. He created the five ages of humanity.

The First Age

First came the Golden Age, a time when a race of golden people lived in complete happiness. But when they died, the earth was again lifeless.

The Second Age

Then Zeus made the Silver Age, when foolish people made of silver quarreled. Zeus grew tired of them, and he destroyed them all.

The Third Age

Third was the Bronze Age, a time of warriors made of bronze who fought until they had killed each other.

Prometheus, in the center, creates the first human, seen on the right. The goddess Athena stands behind Prometheus, ready to breathe life into humankind.

The Fourth Age

Then came the Heroic Age – the time of the *hero*. These men and women were the first true members of the human race. They were made by Prometheus, a Titan to whom Zeus had turned for help. Prometheus created humans in the likeness of the gods, molded into shape from the soil and water of Mother Earth's body.

Zeus was pleased with the new race. He was happy for them to live on earth, as long as they did not have fire. With fire, they could make weapons, cook food, and bring heat and light into their homes. Zeus did not want them to have this knowledge, because he feared they would use it against him.

Prometheus loved the people he had made and could not bear to see them suffer. He wanted to help them in any way he could, so one night he stole fire from the Olympian gods and gave it to humanity. He carried the fire inside the stalk of a fennel plant. Its dry, white pith burned like the wick of a candle. Zeus went into a rage and chained Prometheus to a mountain far away. Then Zeus and the other gods made a woman called Pandora, whom they sent to earth to punish humanity (see page 23).

The Fifth Age

This is the age that we live in today, created for us by the gods as punishment for learning the secret of fire. We are unworthy descendants of the men and women of the Heroic Age and are troubled by our own weaknesses. We are greedy, cruel and unhelpful.

Prometheus makes the human race, then gives them fire:

"Prometheus molded men out of water and earth and also gave them fire, which, unknown to Zeus, he had hidden in a stalk of fennel. But when Zeus learned of it, he ordered Hephaestus to nail his body to Mount Caucasus. He was kept bound there for many years. Every day an eagle swooped on him and ate his liver, which grew back at night. That was the penalty that Prometheus paid for the theft of fire."

From *The Library*, written by Apollodorus, c. 150 BC.

Ο
Π
Ρ
Σ
Τ
Υ
Φ
Χ
Ψ

ΖΗΘΙΚΛΜΝΞΟΠΡΣΤΥΦΧΨΩ

How do we know about the gods and goddesses?

The ancient Greeks loved to tell stories about their past, like this one about the creation of the world. It is just one of many stories that have survived from ancient times. No one knows when the stories were first told, but they were already old by the time they came to be written down. Greek writers, such as Homer and Hesiod, were among the first to record the stories of old Greece.

If they had not been written down, we would not know the stories, since all memory of them would have been lost when the last of the ancient Greeks died.

This portrait of Homer, carved from stone, was made hundreds of years after he had died, when no one could remember what he really looked like. His eyes are closed to show that he may have been blind.

Homer

Although he is perhaps the greatest of all Greek poets, very little is known about the mysterious Homer. He may have lived about 750 BC, and he may have been blind. Two of the finest of all stories are said to have been written down by him – the *Iliad* and the *Odyssey*. They describe events that the ancient Greeks believed happened during the Heroic Age, when heroes lived on earth and fought a great war against the Trojans, the enemies of Greece.

Hesiod

Hesiod was a poet who lived about 700 BC. His long poem, called *Theogony*, or *Birth of the Gods*, describes the creation of the world, the birth of the Olympian gods, and the making of humankind.

Greek storytellers

Storytellers, or *bards*, memorized the myths and legends of ancient Greece and passed them on by word of mouth for hundreds of years. They recited or sang stories and poems at public meetings.

In the ancient Greek language, storytellers were called *rhapsoidoi*, which means "song-stitchers." Their skill was in telling a story in a new way, literally "stitching" it together as they went along, without changing its meaning. A storyteller spoke or sang in a flowing rhythm, which helped make the story more interesting to listen to. Our word "*rhapsody*," which can mean "a patching or stringing together of poems," comes from the old Greek word *rhapsode*.

How do we know what the gods and goddesses looked like?

The Greeks were masters of art. They made statues from stone, metal and wood. They decorated buildings with wall paintings, and they painted pictures on the sides of pottery vases.

Although most objects made of wood rotted away long ago, and not many wall paintings have survived, many objects of stone, metal, and pottery are nearly as good today as when they were made, more than 2,000 years ago.

It is because the ancient Greeks made statues and paintings that we are able to find out what life was like in ancient Greek times. We can see what the ancient Greeks themselves saw, and this helps us to learn about their gods and goddesses. Without statues and paintings to guide us, it would be hard for us to imagine how the Greeks thought their gods and goddesses looked.

A figure of a bard, painted on the side of an *amphora*, a two-handled vase used to hold wine. He stands on a platform, from where he recited a poem or a story to anyone who wanted to listen. This bard is reciting the opening words from Homer's *Iliad*.

The opening words of the *Iliad*:

"The wrath of Achilles is my theme ... which of the gods caused Agamemnon, King of Men, to quarrel with Achilles?"

The ancient Greeks believed that Homer's *Iliad* was their greatest work of literature. It is the story of the *Trojan War*, in which the Greek hero Achilles fought and killed Hector, a hero of the city of Troy.

Π
Ρ
Σ
Τ
Υ
Φ
Χ
Ψ

Λ Μ Ν Ξ Ο Π Ρ Σ Τ Υ Φ Χ Ψ Ω

2 The Gods of Olympus

In Hesiod's poem *Theogony*, we learn of the ancient Greeks' belief that the new gods, the Olympians, overthrew the gods of old, the Titans. From their heavenly home, high up on Mount Olympus, the Olympians kept watch over humankind.

A religion of many gods and goddesses

The ancient Greeks believed in many gods and goddesses. The most important ones were the Olympians – six gods and six goddesses – who were often simply referred to as the Twelve. There were many lesser gods too.

The six Olympian gods

Apollo was the son of Zeus. He was the god of the sun, truth, music, poetry, dance and healing. In times of war, the bow (as in bow and arrow) was his symbol. In times of peace, it was the lyre, on which he made music.

Ares was the son of Zeus and Hera and was disliked by them both. He was the god of war. To the Greeks, he was cruel and bloodthirsty.

Hephaestus was the son of Hera. He was the god of fire, volcanoes, blacksmiths and craft-workers.

Hermes was the son of Zeus. He was the god of travel, business, weights and measures, and sport. He was the messenger of the gods and guided the souls of the dead to the Underworld.

Poseidon was the brother of Zeus. He was god of the sea, earthquakes and horses. The trident was his symbol.

Zeus was the king of the gods and goddesses. He was the god of the weather, and the thunderbolt was his symbol.

A life-size bronze figure of a god, often thought to be Poseidon, the ruler of the seas. In his right hand he may have held a trident, though this has not survived.

The six Olympian goddesses

Aphrodite was married to Hephaestus. She was the goddess of love and beauty.

Artemis was the daughter of Zeus. She was the goddess of the moon, wild animals and childbirth.

Athena was the daughter of Zeus, born from his head. She was the goddess of war, wisdom and art.

Demeter was the sister of Zeus. She was the goddess of grain and fertility.

Hera was the queen of the gods and goddesses, and sister of Zeus, to whom she was married. She was the goddess of women, marriage, and childbirth. All women worshiped her.

Hestia was the sister of Zeus. She was the goddess of the hearth (fireplace), which was the symbol of the house.

The most beautiful goddess of all was said to be Aphrodite. A story tells how she was born from the foam of the sea. The island of Cyprus was said to be her birthplace.

In time, the god **Dionysus** (son of Zeus) became popular, and he took Hestia's place among the Olympians, upsetting the balance of six gods and six goddesses. He was the god of wine and theater.

Family tree

The gods and goddesses were all closely related to each other. Below is a simplified family tree, based on the account given by Hesiod in his *Theogony*, which described the birth of the gods. Other writers came up with different versions, but Hesiod's is the one followed by most historians today.

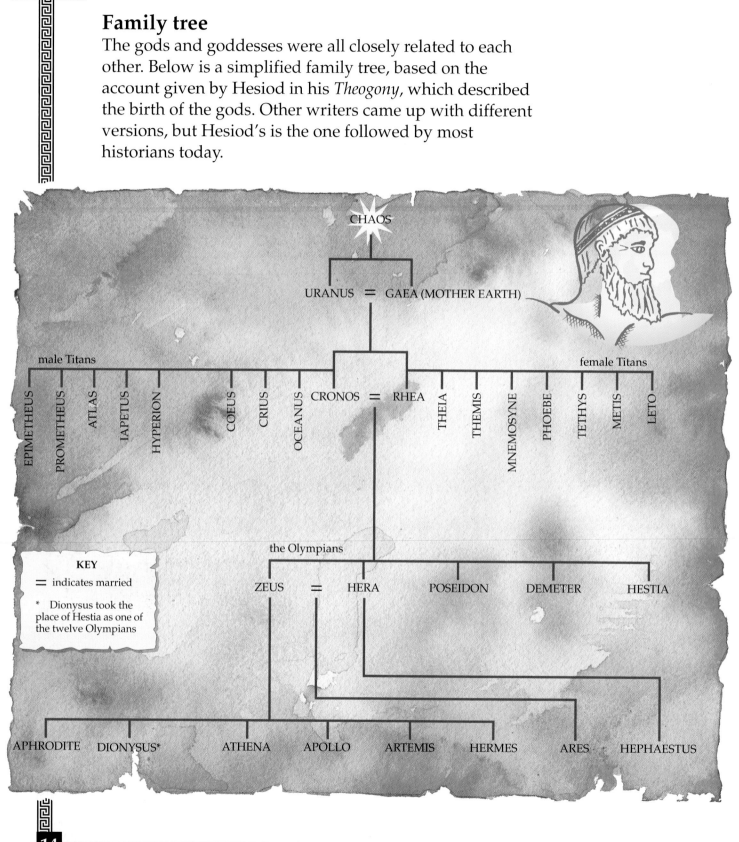

CHAOS

URANUS = GAEA (MOTHER EARTH)

male Titans

EPIMETHEUS PROMETHEUS ATLAS IAPETUS HYPERION COEUS CRIUS OCEANUS

CRONOS = RHEA

THEIA THEMIS MNEMOSYNE PHOEBE TETHYS METIS LETO

female Titans

the Olympians

ZEUS = HERA POSEIDON DEMETER HESTIA

KEY

= indicates married

* Dionysus took the place of Hestia as one of the twelve Olympians

APHRODITE DIONYSUS* ATHENA APOLLO ARTEMIS HERMES ARES HEPHAESTUS

Mount Olympus

The snow-covered Mount Olympus, its summit shrouded in clouds, rises in the Olympus range of mountains in northern Greece. Why did the Greeks decide that this lonely mountain, far away from their major cities, should be the home of their gods? The answer may be that they thought it lay at the boundary of the world, at the very point where the world of mortals ended and the realm of the immortal gods began.

Zeus as the supreme being and god of the weather:

" … the loud-crashing Earth-Shaker, and wise Zeus, father of gods and men, by whose thunder the wide earth is shaken."

From the poem *Theogony*, written by Hesiod, c. 700 BC.

ΙΚΛΜΝΞ ΟΠΡΣΤΥΦΧΨΩ

Mount Olympus is the tallest mountain in Greece. With its top covered in snow and cloud for much of the year, it is not difficult to see why the Greeks made it the home of Zeus, who was also the god of the weather.

Lesser gods and spirits

The Olympians were given the most important place in ancient Greek religion. However, the ancient Greeks worshiped many lesser gods and spirits, too. These included gods that were close to nature, representing rivers and springs, mountains and trees.

Among the spirits were nymphs, who were shy, secretive creatures – a little like fairies. They represented the beauty of nature, and included the Naiads, who were nymphs of streams, and the Dryads, who were nymphs of trees.

Helios was one of the lesser gods. He was the sun god, who rode through the sky in a chariot. Around his head are rays of sunlight.

The Graces and the Muses

The three Graces sang and danced for the gods. They were Splendor, Mirth, and Good Cheer. The nine Muses were the goddesses of the arts – history, astronomy, tragedy, comedy, dance, epic poetry, love poetry, lyric poetry, and song.

Zeus – the father of gods and men

Both Homer and Hesiod called Zeus "the father of gods and men" to show that he was the ruler of all other gods and goddesses and that he was the creator of humankind. He was the supreme being.

Zeus was the god of weather, able to throw thunderbolts down from heaven to strike the earth. It was because he could control the weather that Hesiod called Zeus the "cloud-gatherer," "earth-shaker" and the "thunderer." Controlling the weather meant being in charge of the fertility of the soil, and because Greece was a nation of farmers, good weather was essential, which is why Zeus was such an important god.

On the left of this vase painting sits Zeus. Emerging out of his head is his daughter Athena, armed with helmet, shield and spear. To the right stands Eileithyia, who protected women in childbirth. In this case she is protecting a man.

The birth of Athena

A story about Zeus describes how he gave birth to his daughter Athena. His first wife was Metis, whose name meant "wisdom." Zeus was told their first child would be a girl but that if Metis ever bore him a son, that boy would live to overthrow him.

In the same way that Cronos had swallowed his children to protect himself, Zeus did the same. He opened his mouth and swallowed Metis, together with their unborn daughter. This was the only way Zeus could be sure that Metis would never give birth to a son.

Some time later, Zeus had a terrible headache. He felt that his skull was going to burst open. Realizing what was happening, Hephaestus cut Zeus' skull open with his axe, and from the opening came Athena, the goddess of war and wisdom. She was always Zeus' favorite child.

Athena was the patron goddess of the city-state of Athens. The olive tree was sacred to her, as was the owl, a sign of her wisdom. Her portrait was used on silver coins made in Athens.

3 Temples and Gifts for the Gods

In the early days of ancient Greece, people believed that in certain features of the landscape, such as springs, wells, groves, rocks, and caves, helpful spirits lived. It was important to keep them happy, so shrines were built where people could pray and leave gifts to please these spirits.

As time passed, religion became a greater part of everyday life, and the idea of having a family of gods and goddesses grew in people's minds. It was these supernatural beings, and especially the Olympian gods, who protected and looked after humankind. Out of this belief, came the stories told by Homer, Hesiod and other ancient Greek writers.

The temple to the god Apollo at Delphi was the most famous of all Greek shrines. Pilgrims traveled here from all over the Greek empire until its famous oracle was shut down by the Romans in AD 390.

To please the gods, the old, simple shrines were replaced by temples, which were at first made of timber. And because people wanted the gods to stay and live among them, the temples were built in the same shape as people's houses. Eventually, the wooden temples were replaced by grander ones built of stone, many of which can still be seen throughout the Greek world.

A house for a god

A temple was a house for a god or a goddess to live in. A typical temple site was made up of the following parts:

- a wall that surrounded the whole area.
- an entrance gateway through the wall.
- the sacred enclosure, which lay inside the wall.
- the altar at which *sacrifices* were made.
- the temple building.

Inside the temple building was a large room called the *cella*. In this room was a statue of the god or goddess, which faced the entrance doorway so it could "see" the ceremonies performed outside at the altar.

The temple was quite plain inside, but outside was another matter. Most pilgrims who came to the temple did not enter the building itself, as they made their offerings at the open-air altar in the sacred enclosure. The inside of the temple was a dark and gloomy place, as there was little reason to decorate it. Instead, the outside of the building was decorated with statues painted in bright colors. It must have been a spectacular sight for worshipers to see.

The Parthenon temple at Athens is almost 2,500 years old. Inside was a huge statue of the goddess Athena.

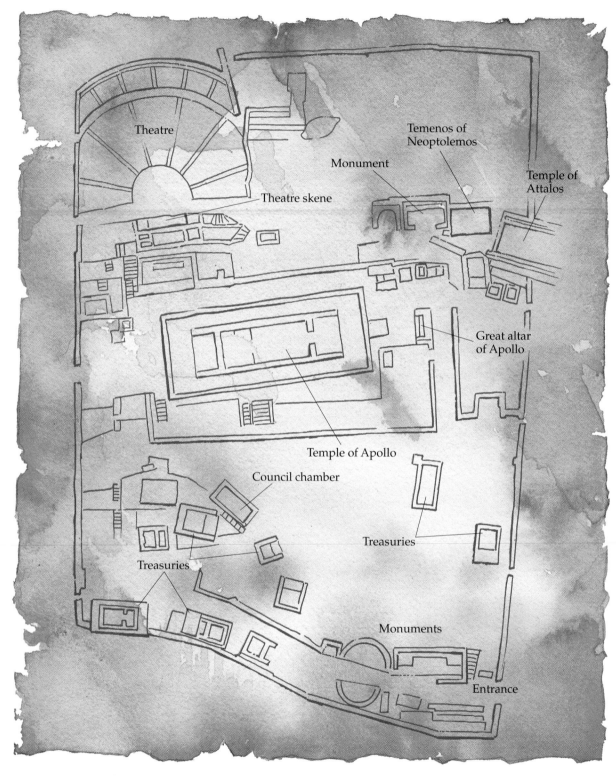

Theatre

Temenos of
Neoptolemos

Monument

Temple of
Attalos

Theatre skene

Great altar
of Apollo

Temple of Apollo

Council chamber

Treasuries

Treasuries

Monuments

Entrance

This is a map of the temple of Apollo at Delphi showing how it was
surrounded by a cluster of other buildings. See photo on page 18.

Gifts for the gods

The greatest gift a person could give the gods was an animal, which was sacrificed on the temple altar. A sheep was the usual sacrificial animal, but an ox pleased the gods more. Most of the time, people were happy just to leave offerings of food, anything from a few grains of barley to complete meals. Wine was used in ceremonies and was poured at the altar. Other types of offerings were items of clothing, locks of hair or pieces of pottery.

No matter how great or simple the offering a person gave, everyone had the same purpose in common – the wish to please the gods in return for their own protection. An ancient Greek proverb said: Gifts persuade the gods.

What to do at a ceremony

Although the ancient Greeks had priests, it was not essential for these priests to be present at every religious ceremony. People were free to contact the gods themselves, at altars in their own homes and at the temples, too.

A young woman offering gifts to the gods. Kneeling and with her head bowed, she is shown in the act of worship.

A description of an animal sacrifice:

"Then, when they had prayed and had sprinkled the barley grains, they drew back the heads of the oxen and cut their throats, then skinned them and cut out their thighbones and covered them with fat. And the old man burned them on stakes of wood ... and when they were burned, they cut up the rest of the meat and roasted it on the fire."

From the poem *Iliad*, written down by Homer, c. 750 BC.

ΑΒΓΔΕΖΗΘΙΚΛΜΝΞΟΠΡΣΤΥΦΧΨΩ

A painting of a sheep being taken for sacrifice. A priest leads the way, carrying wine and a tray of tools for use in the ceremony. Musicians walk behind, followed by worshipers holding olive branches.

Other than leaving gifts of food, wine, and personal objects, these are the other duties people carried out when they wanted to talk to the gods:

- **Prayer**. A worshiper stood before an altar with one hand raised to attract the god's or goddess's attention. The worshiper might offer a prayer of thanks or speak a curse (a hostile prayer), asking the god to send bad luck to someone.

- **Washing**. A worshiper had to cleanse with water before praying. Otherwise, the gods and goddesses would "spit back their prayers," said Hesiod.

- **Burning incense**. The gods liked the smell of *incense* burned at their altars.

What a philosopher said about sacrifices:

"There are three reasons why we sacrifice to the gods: to show them honor, to give them thanks, or to ask for their help."

Theophrastus, c. 300 BC.

ΥΦΧΨ

ΑΒΓΔΕΖΗΘΙΚΛΜΝΞΟΠΡΣΤΥΦΧΨΩ

4 How Jealousy Made Mischief

Prometheus had been good to humankind, for it was he who took fire from the Olympians and gave it to the human race. The gods and goddesses were angry. They feared people would forget them, and with fire, they would learn how to lead better lives. They would want nothing from the gods. And so the gods made Pandora and sent her to earth to punish humankind.

Pandora (middle, top row) whose name meant "All Gifts," receiving her gifts from the gods before being sent off to punish the human race for learning the secret of fire.

Pandora's box

The gods gave Pandora a weakness, that of curiosity. In the house where she lived on earth was a box. Locked inside it were the troubles of humankind: diseases, aches, pains, fear, envy, greed and jealousy. Pandora was warned never to open the box – but one day her curiosity got the better of her and she looked inside.

Out poured the evil contents, and from then on humankind was made to suffer all the things the gods had kept from them until that time. Pandora slammed the lid shut, trapping just one thing inside. It was nothing evil and nothing to fear. It was a blessing. It was the gift of hope for the future, and of better things to come.

What jealousy did to the queen of the gods

One of the things that escaped from Pandora's box was jealousy. Jealousy made people so suspicious of others that they forgot all about the good things in their own lives.

Jealousy visited the gods on Mount Olympus, too, and made mischief among them. Hera, the wife of Zeus and queen of the gods, was jealous whenever he was away from her. He had other wives, too, and they had given him more children, but Hera wanted Zeus all to herself.

One day, Zeus visited the earth and fell in love with Io. Hera was filled with jealousy, and in a temper, she rushed to Zeus. On seeing her coming, Zeus changed Io into a milk-white cow to hide her from Hera.

The creation of Pandora:

"Zeus made an evil thing for men as the price of fire. He made woman to be an evil to man, with a nature to do harm."

From the poem *Theogony*, written by Hesiod, c. 700 BC.

ΙΚΛΜΝΞΟΠΡΣΤΥΦΧΨΩ

Zeus gives Io to Hera

Hera admired the cow so much that Zeus gave it to his queen, so that it would graze among her herds of cattle on earth.

Poor Io. After Zeus and Hera had returned to Mount Olympus, she found herself trapped inside the body of a beast, forced to eat grass and bellow as other cattle did.

Hera, knowing there was something strange about the cow, sent her servant Argus to guard it. He was an all-seeing monster with one hundred eyes. Zeus wanted to change Io back to a woman, but he knew he could not get past Argus. He sent his messenger Hermes to do his work for him.

As Hermes played a tune on a set of pipes, Argus closed his eyes one by one. When he was fast asleep, Hermes cut off the monster's head and led the cow away.

Hera saw everything. She came to earth in her chariot drawn by peacocks and settled beside the head of Argus, whose hundred eyes became the eyes on the feathers of her peacocks.

The marriage of Zeus and Hera. Zeus holds Hera's wrist, which may have been part of the ancient Greek wedding service.

Io flees into Egypt

Hera sent a fly to sting the cow, which caused it to break free from Hermes. Away it ran until it came to the sea. Over it swam, and to this day that stretch of water is called the Bosphorus, which means "cow crossing." It divides Europe from Asia.

The cow fled into Egypt, where it changed back into Io. To remind her of whom she had once been, cow's horns still grew from her head. In Egypt, Io was worshiped as a goddess, and her son, whose father was Zeus, became that country's first pharaoh.

In Egypt, Io was changed from a cow back into a woman. There she was worshiped as the goddess Hathor, who had the horns and ears of a cow. In this carving, made by the Egyptians, you can see Hathor with cow's ears.

26

Women in ancient Greek society

Unlike the powerful goddesses, ordinary women were thought of as second-class citizens, inferior in every way to men. They were forbidden to own property, could not vote, and did not take part in running a town.

A woman's place was at home, where she spent most of her time. It was her greatest duty to be a good wife to her husband and a good mother to their children. She was also expected to instruct the family's servants who worked in the household as cooks, cleaners and weavers.

When a woman did leave the home, it was usually only to attend a religious ceremony. Women had work to do at weddings, and at funerals they acted as mourners, slapping their chests and wailing.

The role of women in ancient Greek society:

"Go to your house, and busy yourself with your work at the loom, and tell your handmaidens to do the same, for it is men who shall be in charge of fighting."

From the poem *Iliad*, written down by Homer, c. 750 BC.

ΤΥΦΧΨ

Ι Κ Λ Μ Ν Ξ Ο Π Ρ Σ Τ Υ Φ Χ Ψ Ω

The Minoans were people who lived on Crete and nearby islands before the arrival of the ancient Greeks. Perhaps this scene of women at a sacrifice would have been familiar to the ancient Greeks, too. These Minoan priestesses are emptying buckets of blood from sacrificed animals.

5 Festivals

Festivals were held in towns throughout the year. Most were held in honor of the gods and goddesses, but some were to celebrate victories in war. Festivals for the gods and goddesses were to please them and to persuade them to protect the town and its citizens.

All normal work stopped at festival time. It was a holiday, a time for people to relax and enjoy themselves a little. Most festivals were linked to the farming year and were held to bless the fields and crops.

The calendar

The ancient Greeks followed a calendar based on the phases of the moon (new moon, crescent moon, half moon, waxing moon, and full moon). This is called a lunar calendar. Their year was divided into twelve months of twenty-nine or thirty days each, and a month began when the new moon was first sighted in the night sky. The religious year began at the end of June. The first day of each month was new-moon day – the holiest day of the month.

In this painting called *Pheidias and the Frieze of the Parthenon,* the Victorian artist, Sir Lawrence Alma-Tadema, shows ancient Greek people viewing a frieze in the Parthenon. They are admiring a scene that shows people taking part in the Panathenaia festival. (See page 30)

The festival of Thesmophoria

The festival of Thesmophoria was held in Athens, one of the main cities in Greece, each autumn. It was a three-day festival for women only. Thesmophoria was a fertility festival, held to give thanks to the goddess Demeter, and to ask her to bless Athens with food, crops, and healthy children during the coming year.

Preparations for the festival began in the spring, when the women threw piglets into caves and hollows outside the city. Then, on the first day of the festival, the rotten remains of the pigs were dug up, placed on an altar, and mixed with grain. On the second day, the women ate no food, and spent their time sitting or lying on the ground, as if to transfer strength from their bodies into the soil. That night, they shouted insults at each other. Then, on the third day, they scattered the pigs' remains and the grain on the plowed fields.

The goddess Demeter

Demeter, in whose honor the festival of Thesmophoria was held, was worshiped mainly by people who lived in the country. Her favorite daughter was the tragic Persephone, whose father was Zeus. You can read her story on page 38.

On the left is the goddess Demeter, the goddess of food, farming and fertility, giving grain to a prince and telling him to use it to teach men how to grow crops for food. On the right is the goddess Persephone.

The Panathenaia festival

The Panathenaia, or "all-Athenian" festival, was the grandest event in Athens. It honored the birthday of Athena. Once every four years, the Great Panathenaia was held, during which a procession made its slow way to the Parthenon temple on the hill overlooking the city.

At the head of the procession was a wooden ship, dragged along on rollers. Instead of its sail, a woman's woolen tunic hung from the mast. At the temple, the tunic was draped over the sacred statue of Athena, where it stayed for the next four years. The placing of the gown on the figure was the most solemn part of the festival, after which cows were sacrificed and burned at the altar. The cooked meat was taken back down to the city and shared among the people.

A statue of Athena stood inside the Parthenon temple in Athens. Made from gold and ivory, it was forty feet high. The original statue was destroyed long ago, but enough descriptions of it exist for smaller copies to have been made, such as this one, from Roman times.

This is an artist's idea of how Athena's statue looked inside the Parthenon. Note the tunic held above the statue's shoulders. It was placed there during the Great Panathenaia festival.

A festival for soldiers who died in war:

"Three days before the start of the ceremony, the bones of the fallen are brought and put in a tent, and people make offerings to their own dead. Then there is a funeral procession, when everyone who wishes to joins in. When the bones have been laid in the earth, a speech is made in praise of the dead, after which all depart."

From *History of the Peloponnesian War*, written by Thucydides, c. 400 BC.

Σ
Τ
Υ
Φ
Χ
Ψ

ΑΒΓΔΕΖΗΘΙΚΛΜΝΞΟΠΡΣΤΥΦΧΨΩ

6 Cults, Oracles and Magic

Greek religion had many layers that fit together to make it all work. The main layer was the family of Olympian gods and goddesses, worshiped throughout the ancient Greek world. It was they who "guided" people's lives from birth to death – and in the life that came after death. In the layer below the Olympian Gods came many lesser gods and goddesses, who were not as popular as the Olympians.

The Greeks told stories about a poet called Orpheus. He composed religious poems that he sang while he played his string instrument. People who followed Orpheus said that when he sang the whole of nature gathered around him.

In return for their gifts of prayers and sacrifices, worshipers looked for signs from Heaven in answer to their prayers. Some signs were easy to see. If the gods were pleased, they would make crops grow in the fields. Likewise, a crop that failed to grow was also a heavenly sign. It meant the gods were unhappy and were punishing the people, who knew then that they faced a year with little food until the next harvest came.

Making sense of the signs from heaven was another layer of ancient Greek religious life. This part of ancient Greek religion was where strange things happened.

Cults

A *cult* is a group of people with the same ideas who decide to act together. Cults can arouse strong feelings in people and are usually linked to their religious beliefs.

One cult from ancient Greece was *Orphism*, which took its name from religious poems said to have been written by the musician Orpheus. Followers of Orphism believed in *reincarnation*. They believed that the soul of a dead person lived on after death and was reborn as another living thing, which could be human, animal, or even vegetable. Orphism promised its followers a happy life after death.

Another cult was based around the god Dionysus, who grew so popular that he became one of the Olympian gods in place of the goddess Hestia. In the cult of Dionysus, followers worked themselves into such a state of great excitement by drinking heavily that they believed that the holy spirit of Dionysus came into their bodies.

Dionysus was the god of wine. He was associated with drunken behavior among the followers of his cult. They said that the god came to them as they drank themselves into a religious frenzy.

Oracles

People believed the gods had messengers on earth called *oracles*. Through the oracles, it was possible to find out about the future.

The most famous oracle was at the town of Delphi, where pilgrims visited the sanctuary of the god Apollo. Inside was a priestess who, so she claimed, could talk directly to the god. A pilgrim asked her a question, such as, "Will it be safe for me to travel by sea?" or "Will the crops grow well in my fields?" The priestess went into a trance and asked Apollo the pilgrim's question. The god spoke through her in a strange language. An attendant understood the words of Apollo uttered by the priestess, and he explained the god's answer to the pilgrim.

The Greeks thought that Delphi was the very center of the world. Pilgrims left offerings to Apollo in shrines cut into the rock. Its famous fortune-telling oracle survived until the Christian era when it was closed down by the Romans in an attempt to ban the worship of pagan gods and goddesses.

The oracle at Dodona

A sanctuary at Dodona, in northwest Greece, was dedicated to Zeus. The main feature of the sanctuary was an ancient oak tree. Pilgrims believed Zeus spoke to them through the tree's rustling leaves – his words were interpreted by priests who lived at the sanctuary.

The sanctuary was in use over a long period. One of the first clues we have to its existence is in Homer's poem the *Iliad*, written in about 750 BC. The poem describes how the priests at the sanctuary slept on the ground and had unwashed feet.

A small sheet of lead found at the sanctuary of Zeus at Dodona. On it is written a question to the oracle, in which a group of people from the island of Corfu ask Zeus to which god or hero they should offer sacrifices to govern their land in the best way.

Apollo, whose sanctuary was at Delphi, was the god of truth. He was famous because he could see the future. On this decorated dish, he is shown pouring wine as an offering. The black raven is a symbol of the future.

King Croesus

To the east of Greece was the land of Lydia, where a king called Croesus ruled. Though he was not a Greek, he believed in the power and the wisdom of the Greek gods. King Croesus wanted to expand his empire by defeating the mighty Persians, who were his neighbors. He would then add their land to his own.

Croesus wanted to know if the gods would be on his side if he attacked the Persians. He believed the oracle at Delphi would guide him in his quest for glory. He sent messengers to Delphi to offer gifts of gold and silver from Croesus to the temple of Apollo. Then they asked the king's question: "Should King Croesus make war on the Persians?"

The priestess at the temple of Apollo went into a trance, during which time she met Apollo and put the question to him. The god answered through the priestess, who spoke in strange, unfamiliar words. When her attendant explained what they meant, the god's answer was: "Yes, if your king fights the Persians, a mighty empire will fall."

The messengers reported the news to Croesus, who believed Apollo had said he would be victorious in battle. But he was wrong, for it was not the empire of the Persians that fell, but his own, as he was defeated in the battle that followed.

A king visiting the priestess at the sanctuary of Apollo at Delphi. The priestess would inhale a vapor and go into a deep trance. Then she was able to cross over into the world of the gods.

Magic and superstition

Magic and superstition were part of everyday life, in much the same way that the gods and goddesses were. For example, the poet Hesiod gives a long list of things that he warns people never to do, for fear of upsetting the gods. Here are four of his superstitious warnings:

- Never cross a river until you have prayed and washed your hands. Whoever crosses with dirty hands will upset the gods, who will bring trouble upon him afterwards.
- Never lay the wine ladle across the mixing-bowl at a drinking party, for bad luck is attached to that.
- Eat nothing from unblessed pots, for in them there is mischief.
- Never pass water in rivers or springs: it is not well to do this.

Pythagoras

Pythagoras, a famous mathematician and philosopher, formed a society whose members followed rules based on superstition. One rule was not to eat beans, since a cut-open bean looked like a human baby in the womb, and to eat it would be cannibalism. It was believed that beans possessed human souls. Believers said that burping was the sound the souls made as they tried to escape!

"A man should not clean his body with water in which a woman has washed, for there is bitter mischief in that."

From *Works and Days*, written by Hesiod, c. 700 BC.

Τ Υ Φ Χ Ψ

ΘΙΚΛΜΝΞΟΠΡΣΤΥΦΧΨΩ

7 The Girl Who Lived in Both Worlds

It was the gods and goddesses who breathed life into our bodies made from the soil and water of the earth. It was they who gave humanity the secret of fire, although they did not want us to know it. And it is the gods and goddesses to whom we offer prayers and gifts, in the knowledge that, one day, they will judge our souls as we enter the life that comes after death. Until that day comes, we all remain as mortals, except for Persephone, forever trapped between this life and the next.

Hades

Hades was the brother of Zeus and Poseidon. When the world was divided between the gods, Zeus had taken the best part and became god of the sky. Poseidon took the next best and became god of the sea. Hades was left with the worst part – all that lay under the earth. This explains how he became god of the *Underworld*.

Persephone was the beautiful daughter of Demeter, the goddess of grain and fertility. Hades wanted Persephone to be his wife and rule over the land of the dead as his queen.

Demeter, fearing for her daughter, took her far away from Greece, to the island of Sicily, where she hoped Hades would not find her.

"A gloomy place is Hades, as far distant from earth as earth is distant from the sky."
From *The Library*, written by Apollodorus, c. 150 BC.

ΙΚΛΜΝΞΟΠΡΣΤΥΦΧΨΩ

Υ
Φ
Χ
Ψ

One day, as Persephone was gathering flowers, she saw a bloom unlike any she had seen before. She knew she must have it, but when she picked it, the ground shook and trembled beneath her feet.

The ground opened. As the gap grew wider, Hades appeared before her in all his deathly darkness and pulled her down to join him as his wife.

Demeter asks Zeus for help

Demeter looked for Persephone but could not find her. While she searched the earth, she could not tend to her fields. Crops failed and people starved. It was only when Helios, the sun god, told Demeter that he had seen Hades take Persephone that she finally discovered what had happened to her daughter. Demeter was angry with the other Olympian gods and goddesses for letting such a terrible thing happen to her favorite daughter.

Persephone stands before Hades in the Underworld.

Zeus, who was Persephone's father, tried to comfort Demeter, but she refused to listen and said the earth would remain without food until her daughter was brought back to her.

Zeus's messages

First, Zeus sent Hermes, his messenger, to Hades. Zeus ordered Hades to return Persephone, saying that if he did not, the gods would be no more. Then, Hermes took a message to Demeter, saying that Persephone would be returned to her on one condition – that, for as long as she had been in the Underworld, Persephone had not eaten any of the food of the dead.

Hades agreed that Persephone could return to her mother, thinking that she had not eaten any food. But a gardener who worked for Hades came forward and told how, one day, he had seen Persephone pick a pomegranate from a tree and eat seven seeds from it. She had eaten the food of the dead!

Persephone's fate

Demeter, angry that her daughter could not return, refused to let the crops grow in the fields. The gods were worried and knew they must act. And so it was agreed that Persephone should live in both worlds. For four months of the year, she would live in the Underworld as its queen, and the rest of the year she would live on earth with her mother Demeter.

Persephone holding the pomegranate from which she ate the seven seeds.

Hades, seen here lying on
a couch with Persephone.
The ancient Greeks didn't
think of Hades as evil. To
them, death was a natural
part of life.

How Persephone was taken by Hades:

*"Persephone was gathering flowers in a soft meadow — roses and crocuses
and beautiful violets, irises, hyacinths and the narcissus — and there grew
a marvelous flower with a hundred blooms. She reached out to take it,
but the earth yawned and opened up, and Hades sprang out and
caught her and carried her away to his kingdom below the ground."*

From the poem *Hymn to Demeter* c. 750 BC.

ΓΣΤΥΦΧΨ

ΑΒΓΔΕΖΗΘΙΚΛΜΝΞΟΠΡΣΤΥΦΧΨΩ

8 The Afterlife

The ancient Greeks believed in life after death. They believed that the souls of the dead left their bodies and traveled to a new life in the Underworld. It was divided into two parts – heaven and hell.

The poet Hesiod described heaven as being above the earth, in the sky where the gods and goddesses lived. He said hell was hidden deep inside the earth. Hesiod said it would take nine days for a blacksmith's anvil to fall to earth from heaven – and nine days for it to fall from the earth into hell. This was his way of saying how far away the two places were.

The ancient Greeks believed that rivers flowed into the Underworld. The river Acheron, seen here, flowed in northwest Greece. Its name means "woeful." Somewhere along its course was an entrance to the Underworld.

A funeral takes place

When someone died, the body was washed and rubbed with olive oil. A small coin was placed inside its mouth. Finally, it was covered with a cloth. The house was cleaned, and wreaths of laurel and myrtle leaves were hung inside. The family sang a sad song, then at night the body was taken to the cemetery, which lay outside the town.

After burial, the grave was filled with soil, and a mound of earth was piled on top. A grave marker, which could be a vase, a statue, or a stone, was placed on the mound. The ancient Greeks believed that the body lived inside the grave, while the soul was taken on a journey to a new life in the Underworld.

The journey to the Underworld

After a dead person had been buried, the soul was taken on a journey by Hermes, the messenger god. He took the soul to the banks of the *River Styx*, the boundary between the world of the living and the world of the dead. Waiting there was a ferryman called Charon. It was his job to row souls across the river, which they paid for with the coins from inside their mouths.

Once on the other side, the gloomy and frightening god Hades – whose name meant "the Unseen One" – took them into a place of reward or of punishment – depending on how good or bad they had been on earth. A three-headed guard dog, Cerberus, stood at the entrance to the Underworld to stop souls escaping.

Greek heaven – the Elysian Fields

People who had lived good lives went to a place of reward. This was the *Elysian Fields*, also known as the Islands of the Blessed. It was a place of parks and fields, where people were happy, surrounded by all the good things they had ever wanted.

Greek hell – Tartarus

People who had lived bad lives went to a place of punishment. This was *Tartarus*, where there was no rest for the wicked. It was a place of constant hardship andpunishment. This was where Zeus had sent the Titans after he had defeated them (see page 7).

Charon, the ferryman who rowed the souls of the dead across the River Styx to their new lives in the Underworld. In the Greek language, *styx* meant "hated." According to the Greek myths, the River Styx flowed around the Underworld nine times.

9 The Legacy

The gods and goddesses, the buildings where they were worshiped, and the stories that were told about them influenced people who came later in history. Their world was still remembered long after the great cities of ancient Greece had fallen into ruins. They left a powerful legacy.

How Greek gods became Roman gods

As the ancient Greek world came to its end, Roman civilization was growing in strength. The homeland of the Romans was Italy, a country to the west of Greece. The Romans created an empire by taking over other people's land. Some lands, such as Greece, were surrendered without a struggle, and most of Greece became part of the Roman Empire in 146 BC.

The Romans learned much from the Greeks. They adopted Greek ideas about architecture, literature and religion. This meant that Greek culture was kept alive throughout the centuries of Roman rule. Many Greek gods and goddesses were taken into the religion of the Romans. They gave them Roman names, but most important of all, they did not change their powers (see page 12 and 13). This meant the same gods and goddesses could be worshiped by both Greeks and Romans, and all that was different was their names. For example, the ancient Greeks called the king of the gods Zeus while the Romans knew him as Jupiter.

GREEK NAME	ROMAN NAME
Aphrodite	Venus
Apollo	Apollo
Ares	Mars
Artemis	Diana
Athena	Minerva
Demeter	Ceres
Dionysus	Bacchus
Eros	Cupid
Hephaestus	Vulcan
Hera	Juno
Heracles	Hercules
Hermes	Mercury
Hestia	Vesta
Pan	Faunus
Persephone	Proserpina
Poseidon	Neptune
Zeus	Jupiter

The major Greek gods and goddesses are shown in **bold** print.

Art and craft

Artists have been fascinated by stories of Greek gods and goddesses for hundreds of years. In Europe, during the fifteenth and sixteenth centuries, artists such as Leonardo da Vinci, Raphael, Michelangelo and others painted pictures in a style that showed their interest in the world of ancient Greece. They painted figures wearing Greek-style clothes and created imaginary scenes from the life of the gods. In art, this time is called the Renaissance.

Architecture – the legacy

In the eighteenth and nineteenth centuries, architects in Europe designed buildings in the Greek Revival or neo-classical style of architecture ("neo" is Greek for "new"). Grand public buildings were often based on the style of ancient Greek temples. They were built to impress people with their size and grandeur – in much the same way as Greek temples had done more than 2,000 years earlier.

Geography

There are many places with links to the myths and legends of ancient Greece. Here are three:

- The **Atlas Mountains**, in North Africa, are said to be where the god Atlas lay down when he grew tired of carrying the weight of the heavens on his shoulders.
- The **Bosphorus**, a narrow strait of water that divides Europe from Asia, is said to be where the goddess Io crossed, disguised as a cow.
- The Aegean island of **Ikaria** is said to be where Icarus fell into the sea after he had flown too close to the sun. Its heat melted the wax that stuck the feathers of his wings together. Ikaria is shaped like a wing – which is why it is linked to the story.

Victorian craftspeople were influenced by the stories of Greek gods and goddesses. Here we see the goddess Demeter, holding a sickle and a sheaf of grain, in her role as goddess of agriculture. She is shown on a wall tile that decorated the inside of a building. It was made about 100 years ago.

Glossary

Amphora
A large pot for storing wine. Its name means "two handled."

Bard
A storyteller who recited from memory stories and poems.

Cella
The innermost part of a temple, where the cult statue of the god or goddess was kept.

Classical
A present-day term that refers to the ancient worlds of Greece and Rome. Artists, architects and craftspeople who base their work on Greek or Roman material are said to be working in a classical style.

Cupbearer
In Greek mythology, Zeus was the cupbearer to Cronos, which meant he acted as a servant, carrying cups of wine to his master.

Elysian Fields
The Greek idea of heaven, where the souls of the dead lived in constant happiness.

Hero
An adventurer who showed great bravery and courage and who was remembered in stories passed on from generation to generation.

Incense
A sweet-smelling vapor made by burning gums and spices, used during religious ceremonies.

Mount Olympus
A mountain in northern Greece where the Olympian gods lived.

Mount Othrys
A mountain in central Greece where the Titans lived.

Myth
A well-known story that has been told for generations.

Nymph
Shy, secretive creatures who represented nature.

Oracle
A temple or shrine where people consulted a god. Pilgrims asked the god a question, and priests interpreted noises as the words of the god.

Orphism
A religious cult in which followers believed in reincarnation.

Reincarnation
The idea that a soul can be born again after a person's death.

Renaissance
The period of European history (c. AD 1400 to c. 1600) when a new interest was shown in classical culture.

River Styx
The boundary between the world of the living and the world of the dead.

Sacrifice
Killing an animal to please a god or goddess.

Tartarus
The Greek idea of hell, where the souls of the dead lived in constant torment.

Thunderbolt
A lightning-flash, thrown from heaven to earth by Zeus.

Trident
A three-pronged spear used for fishing. It was the symbol of Poseidon.

Trojan War
A war between the Greeks and the Trojans, described by the poet Homer.

Underworld
The place of the dead. It was divided into heaven and hell.

Who's Who?

Achilles (A-KILL-EEZ)
Greek hero of the war against the Trojans.

Aphrodite (AFF-RO-DIE-TEE)
Goddess of love.

Apollo (A-POL-O)
God of the sun, truth, music, poetry, dance and healing.

Ares (AIR-EEZ)
God of war.

Argus (ARE-GUSS)
Monster with 100 eyes.

Artemis (ARE-TEE-MISS)
Goddess of the moon, wild animals and childbirth.

Athena (A-THEE-NA)
Goddess of war, wisdom and art.

Atlas (AT-LASS)
An old god, one of the Titans. A giant with great strength.

Cerberus (SER-BER-US)
Three-headed monster dog that guarded the gates to the Underworld.

Chaos (KAY-OSS)
That which existed before the gods, and from which they were born.

Charon (CARE-ON)
Servant of the gods who rowed the souls of the dead to the Underworld.

Cronos (CRO-NOSS)
King of the Titans, the old gods.

Cyclopes (SY-CLO-PEEZ)
One-eyed giants who gave weapons to Zeus, Poseidon, and Hades.

Demeter (DEM-EE-TER)
Goddess of grain and fertility.

Dionysus (DIE-ON-EYE-SUSS)
God of wine and vegetation.

Dryads (DRY-ADS)
Tree nymphs.

Eros (EAR-ROSS)
God of love.

Graces (GRAY-SES)
Goddesses who danced for the gods.

Hector (HEK-TOR)
A Trojan warrior and hero, killed by Achilles.

Helios (HE-LEE-OSS)
Sun god.

Hephaestus (HEFF-EEST-OSS)
God of fire, volcanoes, blacksmiths and craftspeople.

Hera (HAIR-A)
Goddess of women, marriage, and childbirth. Queen of the Olympian gods.

Heracles (HAIR-A-CLEEZ)
Greek hero with superhuman strength.

Hermes (HER-MEEZ)
Messenger of the gods.

Hesiod (HESS-EE-OD)
Greek poet who lived c. 700 BC in central Greece. His poems told stories of the gods and goddesses.

Hestia (HESS-TEE-A)
Goddess of the hearth.

Homer (HO-MUR)
Greek poet who lived c. 750 BC. His poems told stories of the gods and goddesses, and of the war against the Trojans.

Icarus (IK-ARE-USS)
Foolish boy who flew too near the sun, ignoring his father's advice.

Io (I-O)
Girl whom Zeus fell in love with, and who was changed into a cow by Hera.

Muses (MU-SES)
Goddesses who controlled the arts.

Naiads (NYE-ADS)
Stream nymphs.

Olympians (O-LIMP-EE-ANZ)
The main gods, named after their mountain home, Olympus.

Orpheus (OR-FEE-USS)
A musician who lead a rather sad life.

Further Information

Books about the Greek myths

GODS, MEN AND MONSTERS FROM THE GREEK MYTHS
by Michael Gibson, Peter Bedrick Books 1981
MYTHS AND CIVILISATION OF THE ANCIENT GREEKS
by Hazel Mary Martell, Peter Bedrick Books 1998
THE LEGENDS OF ODYSSEUS
by Peter Connolly, Oxford University Press 1991
GREEK MYTHS AND LEGENDS
by Anne Millard and Cheryl Evans, EDC 1996
TALES OF THE TROJAN WAR by Kamini Khanduri, EDC 1998
THE ILIAD by Ian Strachan, Kingfisher 1997

Books for older readers

MYTHS OF THE GREEKS AND ROMANS
by Michael Grant, NAL 1989
WORLD MYTHOLOGY, second editon, by Donna Rosenburg,
NTC Publishing Group 1994

To contact the author, John Malam, you can e-mail him at:
johnmalam@aol.com

Pan (PAN)
God of shepherds, herds and flocks.

Pandora (PAN-DOOR-A)
The first woman, sent by the gods to punish humankind.

Persephone (PUR-SEFF-O-NEE)
Goddess who lived among both the living and the dead.

Plato (PLAY-TOE)
c. 427–347 BC Greek philosopher who thought about goodness, beauty and justice.

Pleiades (PLEA-AD-EEZ)
The daughters of Atlas.

Poseidon (POSS-EYE-DON)
God of the sea, earthquakes and horses.

Prometheus (PROM-EE-THEE-USS)
A wise and thoughtful Titan who helped humankind.

Pythagoras (PITH-AG-OR-ASS)
c. 570–500 BC Greek philosopher, mathematician and miracle-worker.

Rhea (REE-A)
Queen of the Titans, the old gods.

Titans (TIE-TANS)
The old gods who ruled earth before they were defeated by the Olympians.

Zeus (ZYOOS)
God of the weather. King of the Olympian gods.

Index

Numbers in **bold** indicate an illustration.
Words in **bold** can be found in the glossary on page 46.